Prentice Hall

GRAMMAR AND COMPOSITION

SHAMROCKS
'97

SERIES CONSULTANTS

Grade 6
Joleen Johnson
Curriculum Writer, Office of
Secondary Instruction
San Bernardino City Unified Schools
San Bernardino, California

Grade 7
Ellen G. Manhire
English Consultant Coordinator
Fresno, California

Grade 8
Elizabeth A. Nace
Supervisor, Language Arts
Akron, Ohio

Grade 9
Jerry Reynolds
Supervisor, Language Arts
Rochester, Minnesota

Grade 10
Marlene Corbett
Chairperson, Department of English
Charlotte, North Carolina

Grade 11
Gilbert Hunt
Chairperson, Department of English
Manchester, Connecticut

Grade 12
Margherite LaPota
Curriculum Specialist
Tulsa, Oklahoma

CRITIC READERS

Hugh B. Cassell
Jefferson County Public Schools
Louisville, KY

Mary Demarest
St. Mary's Dominican High School
New Orleans, LA

Judy Luehm Junecko
Leesburg High School
Leesburg, FL

Ruth E. Loeffler
Norman High School
Norman, OK

D. Gay Masters
Salem-Keizer Public Schools
Salem, OR

Laura Moyer
Gloversville High School
Gloversville, NY

Avis Satterfield
Virgil I. Grissom High School
Huntsville, AL

Bonnie Scott
St. Augustine High School
St. Augustine, FL

Margie M. Spencer
S. R. Butler High School
Huntsville, AL

Jeanne Bussiere-Stephens
Phillips Academy
Andover, MA

Marvin Zimmerman
Little Rock School District
Little Rock, AR

George Comer
Gary Public Schools
Gary, IN